Dancing and Ballet

Dancing and Ballet

Olive Ordish

Routledge & Kegan Paul

London, Henley and Boston

First published in 1978
by Routledge & Kegan Paul Ltd
39 Store Street,
London WC1E 7DD,
Broadway House,
Newtown Road,
Henley-on-Thames,
Oxon RG9 1EN and
9 Park Street,
Boston, Mass. 02108, USA
Filmset in Monophoto Univers
and printed in Great Britain by
BAS Printers Limited, Over Wallop, Hampshire
ISBN 0 7100 8880 9

Frontispiece: *Ballet Rambert*: Echoes of a Night Sky.

Contents

'. . . all the business of life is to endeavour to find out what you don't know by what you do'

John Whiting *Marching Song*

Introduction

Most people like to dance

How to find out about your sort of dancing

How to present your discoveries

Thoughts on dancing

The world is full of dancing. Nearly everyone likes to move in time to a beaten rhythm. Rhythm runs through the whole universe from the circling of the stars to the throbbing of our pulses. Perhaps we first grow conscious of it when we hear our mother's heart-beat before we are born. Even a baby too young to stand on its feet bounces up and down to music, waving its little hands. Children play dancing games or skip along the pavement for the sheer love of movement. And how many of us can swear that we never danced all by ourselves to music from the radio or record-player?

You dance at school or in discothèques. Perhaps a touring ballet company is coming your way next month or 'Come Dancing' or 'Top of the Pops' is on television tonight. Morris dancers could be giving a display in your village soon or there may be a musical with dancing at the local cinema. Probably you will be able to think of several other possibilities.

Investigating

You may decide to make a special study of a subject that is connected with dancing — a kind of 'project' with all sorts of illustrations. If you do undertake research of this kind, a little detective work may well reveal that there are several dance clubs in your district, whose existence you never suspected. Each will specialize in a different kind of dancing: ballroom, folk, ballet, Old Time, disco, or national dances of other lands, for example.

Your search may bring you some surprises. Maybe that quiet-looking young man sitting opposite you on the bus is a champion sword dancer, or the girl who served you in the shoe shop yesterday is a member of the best formation dance team in the county.

You can find out about local clubs and activities from the district Education Officer, the Citizens Advice Bureau or the public library. Further information on the kind of dance that interests you can be found in books and magazines, some of which will be listed at the end of this volume. The titles of other books on the same subject are often mentioned in the bibliography at the back of a book. All these will provide you with a useful basis to work from – but your own observation is what matters most. Television can help too – a week never goes by without some programmes that include dancing.

Planning your study

What is your idea of a really interesting project? As much variety as possible, I expect, arranged in a way that will present a vivid all-round view of the subject without ever getting boring. It is worth planning it in advance, but not so tightly that no room is left for a lucky find or a bright new thought.

Do you think it is best to start by giving a general outline of the subject and then lead on to details? Or to catch people's attention by some specially interesting point – like journalists do – and so get them to want more general information? Would you prefer to group facts according to date, place or type?

You could include photographs, drawings and paintings as well as newspaper cuttings, charts, models, maps and programmes. A collage picture of a dancer with bright scraps of material pasted on to represent a typical costume would lend colour to a page. Music is very important, so tape-recordings and copied-down pieces of music should have a place.

Dancing in general is really too wide a subject for a short study. It would be better to choose some special aspect of it such as music and costume, folk dancing, national dances of other lands, ballet, an account of dancing during this or an earlier century, or dancing in films, in your county or in the ballroom.

In the beginning

Primitive dancing and magic

Variations of movement

Greek dancing

Nobody knows exactly when and how dancing first began or what the earliest dances were like. We can make probable guesses by observing the festivals of primitive tribes and looking at the drawings on walls, parchments or vases of ancient Egypt, Greece and other very old civilizations. The pictured figures cannot move, however, or tell us how they got from position a to position b.

Ancient Greeks dancing with the infant god Dionysus.

I wonder if the ape men ever made a rhythmic noise and moved in time with it because they enjoyed it? The first music was probably clapping, drumming, stamping, chanting, or blowing into hollow reeds. Which do you suppose came first, the music or the dance?

It is natural to dance when there is cause for rejoicing, such as a good harvest brought in, a marriage or the arrival of guests. Other strong feelings as well as joy can be expressed by dancing. There are courtship dances, sorrowful movements for the death of a chieftain, fierce dances to whip up a warlike spirit. Many primitive dances are religious, a sort of prayer for rain or other favours, or a representation of myths and stories of the gods. Some American Indians, for example, perform dances in which one man acts the part of a stag, while the others pretend to be the hunters that capture it, hoping in that way to give the gods the right idea.

Magic can play an important part. It is possible to dance oneself into a sort of trance.

No doubt dances were very simple at first with everyone stamping and swaying as they felt inclined, but there are always leaders that other people follow, and particular steps and patterns were probably invented very early. Thus ritual movements — that is to say a fixed order of movements, gestures or words to suit a special occasion — arose and were passed on from generation to generation.

An experiment
You and a few friends might be able to work out how such dances developed. Imagine yourselves to be primitive people and decide what occasion you are celebrating. One beats out a rhythm — a nut shaken in a box will do if you have not got a drum — while the rest make the movements (in a circle or a line?) that they feel will best express the joy, sorrow, fierceness or supplication suitable to the occasion. Will a dance gradually develop? If you managed to do it seriously, it could be an interesting experiment.

Steps, patterns and speed
For dance invention you will have to think about basic steps. To take foot movements first, there is simple stepping forwards,

backwards or sideways. Then there are hops, jumps, turns — you will be able to think of others. Head, arms, hands and body can take part as well.

Think about patterns too. Even by yourself you can make movement patterns on the floor and in the air. When a number of people join in the dance the shapes can become very complicated. Among the most usual patterns are circles, as in Ring o' Roses, processions that wind about the dance space, e.g. the Conga, and two rows of dancers facing one another as in Nuts in May.

Changes of speed can give variety too. Sometimes the rhythm starts at a very slow pace, then gradually becomes faster and faster till the dancers are worked up to a high pitch of excitement, when it slows down again quite suddenly before beginning anew.

Dances of the ancient Greeks

The dancing of the early civilizations was sometimes very expert. The ancient Greeks, for example, were very fond of the theatre, in which there was a great deal of dancing. Some of their tragedies and comedies are still acted after more than 2,000 years. Try to find the names of some of them. What do you suppose makes a play's success last so long?

An important part in these plays was taken by the Chorus, a group of minor actors who danced and chanted a sort of commentary on the action of the play.

Their name came from *choro*, the Greek word for 'I dance'. Some modern English words are descended from old Greek ones, and you will find 'chor' as a part of several words connected with dancing: choreography, for instance. If you look that up in the dictionary, you will find other 'chor' words nearby, although sometimes their meaning has been transferred to singing, because the ancient Chorus sang as well as danced.

Greek vases are often decorated with dancing figures. Some are depicted dressed in wreaths and graceful tunics and playing on pipes, while the comic characters are more often disguised as satyrs with goatish legs and horns.

At the beginning of this century some people were very interested in trying to work out what the Greek dances were really like. So-called Greek dancing became quite a fashion.

See if you can find illustrations of early dancing, Egyptian, Greek or Roman, in your local museum of ancient art and history. Try to imagine the pattern of movement.

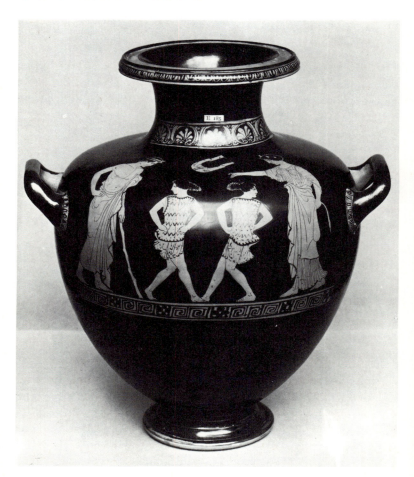

*A Greek vase showing
a dancing lesson.*

Each land its own style

Mysterious East and Rhythmic South, among others

For oneself or for the tourist?

In time the primitive dances became fixed and traditional so that all the people of a particular tribe did them in more or less the same way. Although the steps changed and developed, they did so along the same lines and only very slowly. Thus national styles of dancing arose. I don't know if there are any countries where people do not dance at all. Certainly not many. It is interesting to study the various styles typical of different countries.

Dancing round the world

It is possible to guess the nationality of folk dancers by the steps they perform, even when there is no typical costume to give you a clue. You could easily distinguish between the neat heel-and-toe springing of a Highland Fling, the stamping and proud stance of a Spanish flamenco dance and one of those Russian dances in which the men leap high in the air from a crouching position while the women seem to glide over the ground in tiny steps. I expect you can think of other movements characteristic of a particular country. In what national dances, for instance, do the men stamp noisily with their boots and slap their thighs?

Generally speaking, in European and North American dances the legs and feet do most of the work. In oriental dancing the arms, hands, neck and eyes play the most important part, the feet acting mainly as supports. The 'double-jointed' finger and neck movements that highly skilled Indian dancers can make each have their own special meaning and take years of training. But performers of that quality belong to court, stage or temple and can

hardly be counted among ordinary folk dancers. Have you ever
seen that kind of Eastern dancing? If not, keep an eye on the
television programmes to see if they include any dancing from
India, Bali, Thailand or neighbouring countries. I think you would
find it fascinating.

Javanese dancers.

African dances
Africa is known for the richness and variety of its dancing. It can be
exciting to watch the splendid-looking black dancers, often
dressed in colourful costumes made of such materials as leopard
skin, ostrich plumes and goat skin. Sheepskin leggings or anklets
are very typical. In one kind of dance the man's calf is encircled by
wild fruit shells strung on little sticks that rattle in time to the
dancing, very much like the pads of bells worn round the legs of
our English Morris dancers. Music is supplied by drums, pipes,
xylophones or chanting.

Every tribe has its own style. There are the stamping dances of the
Zulus, the striding dances of the Sotho people, the shaking dances
of the Xhosa, and so on. The pattern may be circular or linear and
there can be different dances for different age groups. Women take
part in some of the dances, and occasionally a sort of clown joins
in as 'comic relief'.

A Nigerian dancing group from the South-Eastern State.

It is generally supposed that some of the Africans sold into slavery in America long ago brought with them their songs and dances, which still survive, greatly changed, in jazz music and some of our modern dances.

Research of your own

You will notice that I have left out descriptions of many countries, even whole continents. That is because you might like to do your own research on them from the beginning.

How about Central or South America, for example? You are sure to have seen Latin American ballroom dancing and heard the exciting rhythm of the music. Mexico, Brazil, Argentina and neighbouring countries have many other dances, not connected with the ballroom. Do you know why the music and dancing in these countries are something like those of Spain and Portugal?

There are also the colourful dances of the West Indies. Have you a West Indian friend who could tell you what a limbo dance is like?

When you are studying a nation's dance there are a number of aspects to consider, including of course the typical steps and patterns and the general effect. What are the names of the principal dances and who performs them: men, women, children, society people, peasants, townsmen, professional dancers, specialists – or everyone? Are special costumes worn? Are there different types of dance in different regions and for various occasions? Above all, what is the music like? A great deal of national dance music can be heard on records. See if you can beat out the characteristic rhythm yourself. Maps and coloured drawings of costumes would make good illustrations.

You might have an interesting discussion with other dance enthusiasts on what most influences the style of a nation's dancing – its history, geography, climate or the character of the inhabitants. Does national costume affect dancing or is it the other way round?

It is not very often that we see folk dancing in quite natural conditions. Interest in the subject and tourism have both increased so much in recent years that what were once a simple part of local merry-making have now become showpieces with expensive costumes and dancing of a professional standard.

There are different points of view as to whether that is a good thing or not. No one can object to the dances being well done, but they may become less genuine when performed only to attract tourists. Could it affect the characters of the people themselves? Does the money it brings in help them or merely enrich others? It is worth consideration.

You may be able to get information about national dances, perhaps with pictures, from the tourist offices or even the embassy of the country in which you are interested.

Folk dances

What exactly *is* folk dancing? The border line between different kinds of dancing is not always quite clear. Primitive dance merges into folk, folk into social or stage dancing, and so on. On the whole it can be said that folk dances come from the ordinary people, who perform them for pleasure. They are traditional: no one knows who invented them, for the movements have been passed down through the generations, changing a little on the way perhaps. Some of the children's games we learnt when very young are good examples. I expect you can think of several of those singing, dancing games.

There has been a great revival of interest in folk music lately. Sometimes a modern song is described as 'live folk' and labelled with the name of the composer. Whether that can be true folk music could be the subject of a lively argument!

4   The British Isles

Our own dances, Scottish, Irish, English, Welsh

English dance revived

The monstrous hobby horse

Men only?

Scotland

The British Isles are rich in folk dances. Perhaps the best known are those of Scotland. We are all familiar with the wild, sad music of the bagpipes and the merry, catchy tunes they play for the dancing. Have you ever done an Eightsome Reel or the Gay Gordons at a party? They are great fun. But to get the best out of them it is absolutely necessary to learn the steps properly and to practise the precision and muscular control they require.

On starting, the feet should be at an angle of 45° to each other. The skipping, hopping and beating steps must be done lightly on the ball of the foot and the knees should not be allowed to come forward. Each dance begins with a bow from the man and a curtsey from the lady. When the dances are for several people there are all sorts of changing patterns, such as lines facing one another, circles with one or two dancers in the centre and so on. Here teamwork is even more important than personal skill. Many of the dances have attractive names such as the Dashing White Sergeant and the Queen's Delight. You might make a collection of interesting titles.

A sword dance in which the dancer has to hop and skip swiftly but carefully between crossed swords is often a solo.

If you play a record of Scottish dance music or even hum one of the tunes and do a few more or less Scottish steps to it, you will feel the exhilaration. Even in England there are quite a number of Scottish Dance Clubs where people who are keen can become really skilled as well as having a great deal of pleasure. I wonder if there is one in your neighbourhood? A member does not need to be Scottish but is expected to acquire the right costume — kilt, etc., — sooner or later.

Can you find out what a ceilidh is? And how to pronounce it?

Ireland

Irish dances have the most lilting tunes. 'Phil the Fluter's Ball' is quite a modern one but makes a splendid accompaniment to an Irish jig. The rapid and precise footwork of an Irish jig is closely related to the Scottish kind. Unfortunately reels and jigs for competition have to be performed in an expressionless way with the arms hanging down, unmoving, at the sides, which gives the dances a rather prim appearance. Towards the end of a village ceilidh you might see them done in a less expert but more carefree and attractive way!

Irish dancing at the Galway oyster festival.

The old folk dances move in elaborate patterns which some scholars have likened to the swirling designs on old Celtic crosses and manuscripts. One ancient peasant dance is called Rinnce

Fada (long dance) and another the Rinnce Mor (big dance). There is a dance in which the couples are linked by the kerchiefs they hold and with which each pair in turns forms arches for the rest to pass under. In fact, there is a wealth of material to study.

Wales
The dances of Wales must once have been as numerous and varied as those of the other British countries, but during the late eighteenth century there arose a popular religious sect that believed dancing to be sinful. The result is that many of the old dances died out and were forgotten. Most Welsh people now regret it and would like to find out more about them. Readers living in Wales might find it interesting to join in the search. They could even discover new information to pass on to the folk specialists. The existence of a dance during which the dancers jump over a candle and of another called Twelve Curtseys to the Moon suggests that there is some fascinating material about.

Old people living in remote places could have interesting memories on the subject. To start you off there are a few books on Welsh folk dancing listed at the end of this volume, and I am sure the experts at the Welsh Folk Museum in Cardiff would be glad to help you.

Every year there is a great Eistedfodd or arts festival held at Llangollen, where you can see folk dancers from many lands.

England
England, too, has a rich variety of folk dances showing signs of their descent from both our Celtic and our Nordic ancestors. But here, as in several other industrial countries, these dances were in great danger of being lost. The Industrial Revolution that began at the end of the eighteenth century sucked country people into the towns. Somehow town life does not seem to encourage folk dancing. Why do you suppose that is? The only true London folk dance I can think of was the one the East-end cockneys used to do round the barrel-organs on bank holidays at the end of the last century, when they wore 'pearlies' and ostrich-feather hats quite naturally on such occasions. Now that the street organs have died out all that is left of that is 'Knees Up, Mother Brown'.

Cecil Sharp and the folk revival

Luckily, before it was too late, a musician called Cecil Sharp became interested in old folk songs. In 1899, when he was spending Christmas with friends in Oxfordshire, a 'side' or team of Morris dancers came to the house and danced on the snow-covered lawn to their own music. The 'squire' or leader said he had learnt it all from his father, who had learnt it in turn from his.

Cecil Sharp was so interested that he spent the rest of his life touring the countryside, discovering all the ancient songs and dances that were still being performed. After some years he had collected and written down a hundred different kinds of jigs and Morrises, twenty-five sword dances, some horn dances and several hundred country dances. Before he died in 1924 he wrote a number of books, started clubs and gave demonstrations.

As a memorial to him his many followers founded Cecil Sharp House in London, the headquarters of the English Folk Dance and Song Society, a splendid place well worth a visit. Among other things it contains a concert hall, fine rehearsal rooms, a music shop and a small museum. There is a library too, not only of books but also of records, where you can find out a great many facts about folk dancing.

The Morris

One fine spring day as you walk through a village or country town you may hear the merry music of pipe and tabor (a small drum) — or nowadays more often an accordian — and a faint jingle of bells. An intent little crowd of spectators blocks your view at first, but soon you see six or more men dressed in white, rather as if for cricket. This is no cricket, however, for they wear crossed ribbons on their chests, pads with little bells tied round their shins and maybe flowers round their hats. They are dancing with light springy steps and waving white kerchiefs. These are the Morris men. Sometimes there is clowning by a hobby horse and a man dressed as a woman (like a pantomime dame) known as the man-woman or Betsy. They are part of a very old tradition often added to the Morris.

It is hard to be sure how the name arose. Some think it is connected with the word 'Moorish' because the dancers used to blacken their faces as a sort of disguise. The dance itself is supposed to be far older than its name and to have had its beginning in the Late Stone Age. No girls or women take part in it.

There are many kinds of Morris dances, mostly found in north-west England, the Midlands and the Cotswold area. Teams and clubs exist all over the country, however, for the members find it an envigorating mixture of dance and sport. See if you can discover when they will next give a display in your district.

The Morris men.

Other dances

Sword dances belong especially to north and north-eastern England, where they used to be performed by groups of miners. The long swords or short 'rappers' are not crossed on the ground as in the Scottish version but intertwined above the dancers' heads. Can you find out in what part of the country Horn Dances take place, and why they are so called?

Every year on 1 May a strange ritual lasting all day takes place at Padstow in Cornwall. A monstrous sort of hobby-horse made of wood and cloth is urged to dance through the day by two men called the teazers, carrying 'clubs'. Every now and then the music slows down and the 'Oss' appears to be dying until the teazers

The Padstow 'Oss, *a Cornish Mayday dance.*

manage to bring it back to life. It is clearly descended from some ancient ceremony of pagan magic, perhaps a fertility rite.

Another Cornish dance consists in a luck-bringing procession winding through the streets and in and out of the houses. Do you know its name, the town where it takes place and the famous tune to which it is danced?

Ideas and projects

There are many other dances belonging to the British Isles, including a special sailor's dance that you probably know. An interesting subject for research would be the dances of your own part of the country. Books would give you a good start and your local museum or 'stately home' may have illustrations of dancing at old festivals and weddings. If you find any interesting evidence of this kind, it is wise to note down the book, picture or other source of information from which it came. Historians always do this in case they are later asked to prove the truth of what they say.

Living evidence and information can also be found in your nearest folk dance club. Best of all, take an active part in the dancing. Every county has its own Folk Dance Society linked with national and international groups and may run dances, folk dancing holidays and join in events abroad.

A study of dancing all over the British Isles, on the other hand, would best be illustrated by a map with different colours showing the main types of folk dance in each area. More detail could be supplied by the addition of place names and 'pin men' or little signs such as crossed swords, horns, etc., to mark special dances. A 'key' at the foot of the page would explain what the colours and symbols mean.

Photographs, drawings and descriptions could be added. What about the music? What instruments are used? Many of the dances go to well-known songs. The three main rhythms are: 6/8 time for jigs, 4/4 time for reels and hornpipes, 3/4 time for waltzes.

Country dances

You may have noticed that most of the dances I have described are for men only. Girls have their fair share in country dances, however. These were for getting together and making merry on holidays and other festive occasions, and so come under 'social dance' as much as 'folk'. They include such dances as Eightsome Reels and Sir Roger de Coverley. The latter is a so-called 'longways dance', in which two rows of dancers face one another, each pair dancing across and becoming 'top couple' in turn. There is great festivity in the description of that sort of country dance in Dickens's *Christmas Carol*.

> Away they all went, twenty couples at once, hands half round and back again the other way; down the middle and up again; round and round in various stages of affectionate grouping; old top couple always turning up in the wrong place; new top couple starting off again as soon as they got there; all top couples at last and not a bottom one to help them. When this result was brought about old Fezziwig, clapping his hands to stop the dance cried out 'Well done!' and the fiddler plunged his face into a pot of porter especially provided for that purpose.

It would be interesting to make a collection of references to dances in books.

Here is one clue for a start: Shakespeare's *Winter's Tale*, IV, iii.

While, as I said, it is not much good going in for Scottish dancing without first practising the steps, English folk dancing can be enjoyed even by a beginner, as long as there is a good 'caller', for it comes as much through feeling as through thought. What would you say were the advantages and disadvantages involved in these two different approaches? Of course practice and skill are needed to get the best out of English dancing too.

Some country dances that fell out of use in the British Isles survived in Canada and the USA and came back to us in the form of Square Dancing during the Second World War. There was quite a craze for it in the 1940s. The 'calling' is particularly amusing and contains some special expressions such as 'dosey-do'. That comes from French. Can you guess what it means?

English country dancing.

It would be a help to your project to find a clear way of explaining the steps and patterns of a country dance in words and pictures — not as easy as it sounds. Try imagining that you have to describe one — 'Oranges and Lemons', for example — in a letter to a friend. You would probably find that you needed little diagrams marked 'figure 1', 'figure 2' and so on as well as a description in words.

Social dance

Dancing at parties, then and now

From pavane to jazz

Describing a disco

A party amusement
By social dancing we mean dancing for pleasure and to meet each other, the sort we do at parties and balls. There have been dances like that for thousands of years, but we have no exact knowledge of how they were done before about 1400. From that date onwards there are documents in existence describing some of the dances, steps and music.

Dances come and go
The fashionable dance in the fifteenth century was the basse dance. *'Basse'* is the French word for 'low' and indicated that the dancers' feet did not quite leave the floor but glided along it. There were seven groups of steps, each known as a 'measure', during which the performers made various patterns on the dance floor, rose on their toes during some steps and did a great deal of bowing and curtseying.

A dancing master of that time wrote that the qualities needed by a good dancer were (a) a sense of rhythm (b) memory for steps (c) a sense of positioning on the floor (d) lightness (e) balance (f) grace. Do you feel that these points are equally right for today, or would you add or subtract any qualities?

After a while the younger people at court grew tired of such stately measures and learnt some livelier dances that they had seen the peasants doing in the country. They adapted them to the ballroom and danced them there, much to the disapproval of some of their elders. But the new steps caught on and became a craze — until they in their turn grew old-fashioned. That is a pattern you will see over and over again in the history of dancing — and of other things as well. Can you think of some examples nearer your own time?

In the days of Henry VIII and Elizabeth I

If you watch historical films or television plays you have most likely seen some dances of the sixteenth century. The English were so fond of dancing then that ambassadors from overseas referred to them as 'the dancing English' in the secret reports they sent home. Do you think the name still applies?

In the days of Queen Elizabeth there was a great craze for a dance called the Volta in which the couple held each other as in a modern waltz, and every now and then the man helped his partner to leap high in the air. Some people thought it very shocking but did not dare to say so when the Queen herself, who was very proud of her dancing, joined in the fun.

Shakespeare mentions this dance in Act III of *Henry V*. See if you can track down the passage. In the same sentence he mentions another dance, the Coranto or Courante, one version of which was described by a dancing master as follows:

> Three men invited three girls to join them in the dance, then each in turn escorted his partner to the end of the room and returned alone. That done, they advanced again 'gamboling and making all manner of amorous glances' to claim their partners' arms, but the girls refused and turned their backs. When they saw their cavaliers leaving them again, however, they looked sad and beckoned them to return. Back came the men, knelt at their partners' feet, the girls fell into their arms, and all danced the Courante pell-mell.

Later on the play-acting was left out and the dance grew slower.

Can you find the names of other dances of the period? Do you know what music was played for them and on what instruments? Examples of these old instruments are to be seen in many museums, especially the Victoria and Albert and the Horniman in London. There are gramophone records of period dance music too.

Dancing time-travel

You can actually see dances from the fifteenth to eighteenth centuries beautifully performed to the right music and in the correct costume, if you are lucky enough to go to a display by one of the societies devoted to re-creating them as they really were. One of these societies is the Nonsuch, another is the Companie of Dansers. The local Education Officer will know if they are planning to give any performances near your home. They might also be interested to hear of young people really keen to join.

A dance of Henry VIII's time, performed by the Nonsuch Dancers.

The seventeenth century

Dancing grew less lively but more organized during the next century. Famous dancing masters wrote books about it and great composers wrote music for it.

Among the English writers were John Weaver and John Playford, whose books can still be found in the larger libraries. Playford was interested in the old English country dances and collected some nine hundred of them in his books. They became a fashion everywhere.

Samuel Pepys, who wrote a famous and amusing diary during the reign of Charles II, has left us this description of a court ball in 1662:

The king led a lady in a single Coranto and then the rest of the
lords, one after another, other ladies; very noble it was and a
pleasure to see. Then to country dances, the King leading the
first . . . he dances rarely, much better than the Duke of York.

Soon the country-dance vogue spread to France, where the name
was changed to the more French-sounding *Contredanse*, and
from there to Italy and Spain.

Nevertheless, it was usually France that set the dance fashions in
those days. King Louis XIV of that country, a powerful and
splendour-loving monarch, was passionately interested in the
subject.

Dress may have had an influence on the style of dancing, for the
women wore long wide skirts, while the men had large wigs on
their heads and wide cuffs on their sleeves. Their short breeches
made it difficult for bad dancers to hide their clumsiness. Have
clothes an effect on today's dances, do you think? You might be
interested in finding out how people dressed during these
centuries. If you are fond of drawing and painting, a picture of one
of the ballroom scenes I have described would make a good
illustration for your project. Otherwise you could hunt for suitable
printed pictures and postcards. The former might be found among
the illustrations in the *Radio Times*, *Dancing Times* etc., the latter
could be looked for at picture galleries or 'stately homes'.

As time went by
Dances came and went. Some were passing fancies, others stayed
in fashion for a long time, gradually changing through the years.
There were Sarabandes, Almaines, Minuets, Polonaises, Gavottes
and many others.

Great composers still wrote music under those headings, but now
the pieces, although composed in the time and sequence of the
dances, were not really meant to accompany them. Among these
musicians were Purcell of England, Scarlatti of Italy, Bach of
Germany and Handel who was born a German but settled in
England. You might see how many sixteenth- to eighteenth-

century compositions you can find under dance names. Radio concert programmes and record catalogues would make good hunting grounds, but it is better to hear the music itself.

Queen Elizabeth and the Earl of Leicester dancing the Volta.

Assemblies

Not all ballroom dancing took place at court or private houses. In the eighteenth and nineteenth centuries there were assemblies — what one might call supper dances today — for people who paid a subscription. Most towns had Assembly Rooms, some quite modest, others large and splendid. Are there any still existing in your area? In some cases they have been turned into warehouses where, perhaps, only some crumbling decoration on the ceiling remains to tell of past glory.

The most fashionable of these gatherings were at Almack's Club in London and the Assembly Rooms at Bath. The latter have been restored and are open to public view.

Authors of the period often used them as the scene of meetings and fallings in and out of love. A great part of Jane Austen's novel *Northanger Abbey* takes place in the Bath Assembly Rooms. I think you would find it an amusing book in any case. It is really

more interesting to read descriptions by writers who actually knew
the place at the time than those by historical novelists who have to
imagine it.

The Waltz

The great dance that burst on the world in the early nineteenth
century was the Waltz. Once an Austrian peasant dance, it became
the rage at fashionable balls all over Europe. Away whirled the
couples, round and round in 3/4 time, actually in each other's
arms, which had been unheard of in a ballroom since the days of
the Volta. People disapproved of course, including that not over-
moral poet, Byron. A writer in *The Times* felt it his duty to 'warn
every parent against exposing his daughter to so fatal a
contagion'.

It was all no use. The Waltz continued to be popular for a hundred
years and is not yet dead. Even the young Queen Victoria danced it
and many composers wrote music in Waltz time. I'm sure you must
have heard the famous Viennese Waltzes 'The Blue Danube' and
'The Merry Widow'. Do you know the names of the two
composers who wrote them?

Dancing and war

During the 1800s, when the Waltz first appeared, the Napoleonic
wars were raging. After the battle of Waterloo, which ended them,
a veritable fever of dancing broke out in Europe, just as it did after
the war of 1914–18. Is there, perhaps, a connection between the
years of stress and anxiety and the spate of dancing that followed
them?

Some thirty years after the Waltz another popular dance for
couples was introduced, the Polka with its gay one-two-three hop
rhythm. For a number of people together there were still the
Quadrille and, later, the Lancers, composed of complicated steps
and figures.

A Victorian ball

Young people did not arrive at Victorian balls in couples. It was not considered correct to dance with the same girl more than four times. Unmarried women were accompanied by an older woman, known as a chaperone, and the girl had a little white card with numbered dances on it. If a young man — who wore white gloves and had been properly introduced of course — asked for a dance, she booked it in this 'programme'. The belle of the ball had every dance taken. When a less sought-after girl had a vacancy she sat, feeling rather humiliated, beside her chaperone and hence was known as a 'wallflower'. That does not happen today when you go in an even-numbered party, though it could if you went by yourself or with a friend of the same sex. On the other hand, at the old balls you never knew whom you might meet or who would ask for a dance — and that could be interesting! Which custom would you prefer?

Things aren't what they used to be

We tend to think that manners in our great-grandmother's day were much more dignified than our own, so it is surprising to hear the opinions of a lady writing about ballrooms in 1890. 'Supper, flowers, palms, etc., are all better than at Almack's in the old days. The electric light is brighter but not so pleasant as the myriads of wax candles there. . . .' But it was not so exclusive, she said, for

An eighteenth-century ball painted by Hogarth.

'that would be impossible today. We live in an age of general levelling up. . . . Men come up to ask for a dance, saying "Have a square? Dance the next round?" What would the courtly lords and ladies of old think of our manners today?'

If we want to know what balls and dances were really like between 1850 and 1940, a very good way is to look at the old bound volumes of *Punch* or the *Illustrated London News* sometimes found at public libraries.

THE TANGO IN THE BALL-ROOM.

AS LETTERS IN THE PAPERS FROM AMATEUR SOCIAL REFORMERS WOULD HAVE US IMAGINE IT.

A Punch *joke about the Tango craze of 1913.*

AND AS WE HAVE ACTUALLY SEEN IT.

Our own century
With the twentieth century came the great explosion of dance
from across the Atlantic. It started with negro music from the USA,
using a new irregular or syncopated rhythm known as ragtime.
Alexander's Ragtime Band first brought it to Britain in 1912. Some
people went mad about it, others could not bear it. But there was
no stopping the flood. New dances were invented, often made up
of walking and turning movements to go with the new beat.

Not all American influence was negro, however. Argentina sent us
the Tango, all smooth glides, swayings, sudden stops and turns.
'Imitate the sinuous grace of the tiger', counselled one writer. In
1913 people were dancing it everywhere, even giving 'tango teas'.
The long narrow 'hobble skirts' of the period were slit up enough
to allow the woman to do the steps. The Barn Dance was the first
American square dance to be imported.

War and jazz
Then came the Great War of 1914–18 that 'put out the lamps all
over Europe' and brought death to so many of the young dancing
men.

Ragtime survived it. All through the war it was developing,
particularly in a certain town in the southern USA that any jazz
enthusiast among my readers will be able to name. 'Jazz' bands
arose, usually made up of special drums, saxophones and a few
other wind instruments. A feature of jazz was the way one player
would suddenly improvise with a variation of his own on the main
theme. The sort of dancing it inspired was called 'jazz' too. By the
1920s jazz had crossed the Atlantic and everyone was doing it. To
its rhythms people danced the Foxtrot, the One-Step, the
Charleston . . . no doubt you can find others.

Dance mania
The post-war dance madness had broken out. There were private
balls, public balls, fancy dress balls, balls at hotels and *thés
dansants*. But now at last dancing on the grand scale also became
available to those without much money to spend. Dance halls and
'Palais de Danse' were opened in all the big towns. For as little as

one shilling (5p) you could dance to the best bands in splendid surroundings — and even hire partners for a little more. The Palais de Danse at Hammersmith and the Empress Rooms at Blackpool were the best known and are still going strong.

But all these were not enough for the young people. At the least excuse they wound up those gramophones that seem so old-fashioned to us now, rolled back the carpet and danced at home.

Within living memory
We have now reached the period that your grandparents can tell you about. Perhaps you can get one of them to demonstrate the dances for you, especially the Charleston!

Your parents will remember some of the dances that came into fashion after the Second World War. They were often called after the sort of music that inspired them — jitterbug, swing, jive, rock 'n roll, or the Latin American rumba, samba and cha-cha-cha.

It was in the 1950s that partners in dances for couples first unclasped and began to dance opposite each other but separately. Does it strike you as strange that in what is called a 'permissive age' they have at last given up a custom that so shocked the prudes 150 years ago?

Projects
If you are considering a study about dancing in any historical period, it might be helpful as well as interesting to make a sort of chart with columns headed 'date', 'name of dance', 'remarks', and so on. Historical dates are often supposed to be boring. Personally, I must confess that I am rather fond of them, because they help one to tie things up and imagine the sort of buildings, costumes, manners and events that formed the background of the period you are dealing with.

There is no reason why you should not make today's 'popular' or 'disco' dancing the subject of a project. Who is in a better position to do that than yourself?

You probably dance at local clubs or discothèques already. Do it now with super-observant eyes! Make notes on steps, customs, manners, music, dress and types of dancer, as if you wanted to convey them all to a future generation to whom they are unknown. Watch TV programmes such as 'Top of the Pops', study the different places where people dance, find out how the dances developed and if they are done differently in other countries. Perhaps your manuscript will be discovered a hundred years hence and used as valuable evidence!

6   Ballroom and stage

In the ballroom

Going in for competitions

Stage, film and television

Ballroom dancing

In spite of the new sort of dancing mentioned at the end of the last chapter, there are many people who prefer the older styles, known as ballroom dancing. These, too, have undergone a certain amount of change during the years.

Organization

As early as the 1920s dance teachers had formed an association which grew into the Official Board of Ballroom Dancing. Many other groups are recognized by the Board, for example the Northern Counties Dance Teachers' Association and the Scottish Dance Teachers' Alliance as well as the International Dancing Teachers' Association. Is there one for your part of the country?

To keep up and improve the standard of dancing they hold conferences, arrange demonstrations, set examinations and sponsor competitions. There are competitions for all levels: under-twelves, under-sixteens, adults, amateurs and professionals. You can join a class or club and, if you choose, try to achieve bronze, silver or gold medal standard and other grades.

What are the advantages of this highly organized grading? Would you rather learn with or without it?

Formation dancing

You might like to go in for formation dancing, in which a number of dancers move through changing patterns on the ballroom floor. For that you have to join a club or class and become part of a team.

Champion ballroom dancers, Dennis Udell and Joyce Brampton.

It is great fun, but it must be remembered that here co-operation is more important than personal skill. Missing regular practice means letting the side down.

Other offshoots of ballroom dancing you might like to investigate are Old Time and Modern Sequence, which have organizations of their own.

'Come Dancing'
To see ballroom dancing at its peak, watch the regional, national and international championships, which can be really exciting. They are often shown on television in such programmes as 'Come Dancing'. You will see such dances as fox-trots and waltzes as well as Latin American and formation dancing.

The dancers, you will notice, wear special clothes for the occasion: more or less the party fashions of the 1950s when men dressed in 'white tie and tails' and women wore full and often spangled skirts reaching halfway between knee and ankle. These clothes are on the way to becoming 'folk costume', but are not entirely without purpose. The men's evening suits give them an elegance they might not otherwise possess. The women's swirling skirts are short enough to show off their grace and amazingly precise footwork — or long enough to conceal their faults! What are your views on these costumes?

Latin American dancing by champions David Douglas and Janice Barb.

Some of the steps used in championships are almost like those of stage dancing or ballet. To reach these heights requires not only a certain amount of money but also a great deal of time and hard work. Four hours' practice a day is not unusual. And then there is the question of finding the right partner.

The 'English Style' is the leading one throughout the world at present, and British couples win most of the championships. Beware, however, for the Japanese and others are after them and getting better all the time! So who will get ready to dance for his/her country?

Dancing for pleasure

But it must be remembered that this competitive dancing is for the few and gives a false idea of the ordinary ballroom kind which can be enjoyed by anyone and does not demand a special sort of clothing nor an unreasonable amount of time and money.

Local dancing schools usually offer inexpensive lessons to teenagers. It is worth enquiring. Most dance teachers are willing to discuss the subject and perhaps let you watch. One can learn a lot from being an observant wallflower!

Note, for instance, how the partners hold their arms and hands. Are the feet kept parallel or pointed outward? In which direction does the man generally face? Notice whether the dancer looks as if he were enjoying himself or as if he were earnestly counting 1, 2, 3, turn. . . . It is so important to listen to the music, but some people forget.

What makes a good dancer do you think? One professional dancer said that the three chief qualities needed were 'technique, poise and grooming'. You may well not agree. How would you define the word 'technique'?

The press

Local newspapers can be a useful source of information. There are nearly always advertisements for dance clubs and schools, dinner dances, mobile discos and so on, as well as announcements of dancing examination results. For deeper research there are specialist journals (see back of this book).

You will often notice the initials IDTA after the name of a ballroom dancing teacher. Find out what the letters stand for when they are advertised. Are some of the initials used in this way more valuable than others?

A debatable point

An interesting subject for discussion might be 'which offers better possibilities, ballroom or disco dancing?' One is more sociable, the other more independent. Both, at their worst, can degenerate into a dull sort of jog.

Stage dancing

'Stage dancing' is rather difficult to define. It is not the same as classical ballet. Perhaps one could say it was any other sort of dancing performed in a theatre, film or television production to entertain an audience. Stage dancers today need a full ballet training and often go in for acrobatic and tap dancing as well.

Chorus girls
Fifty years ago it was not so strenuous. The pretty 'chorus girls' in revues and musical comedies in those days were only required to perform simple steps and high kicks all together on the same beat — though even that is not as easy as it sounds. Try it with a friend!

The most famous were the beautiful Gaiety Girls of London's Gaiety Theatre before the First World War. Their adorers, known as stage-door Johnnies, gathered nightly to see them emerge from the theatre. Quite a number of the girls married lords and millionaires. Nowadays dancers in 'musicals' need not be quite so beautiful, but they have to dance better.

In living memory
Of course professional dancing is as old as civilization and there are records of it going back to ancient Egypt and Rome. But here we will begin with the rapid improvement in stage dancing that occurred within living memory.

In 1974 a film called *That's Entertainment* was released. It contained clips from a great many musicals of the 1930s, 1940s and 1950s. Among the dancing stars was the unique Fred Astaire, now an elderly man but then a young faunlike creature, light as air and very amusing. He was a perfectionist who rehearsed for long hours and took infinite trouble to see that everything connected with his act was faultless. Yet to see him spring lightly from floor to drum to table, doing a nimble tap on each of them you would think he had just invented the steps on the spur of the moment. He would be a good subject for a biographical sketch. There has been a revival of interest in him lately. Books have been written about him and his songs are often broadcast. There is 'Puttin' on my Top Hat', for instance, and 'Dancing Cheek to Cheek'. You may be able to think of some others with the words 'dance' in the title. Who were his best-known partners?

Rather later came the dancer Gene Kelly with his 'Singin' in the Rain' song of 1952.

Fred Astaire.

The great American musicals
During the 1940s and 1950s a stream of vigorous 'musicals' flowed from the USA. The songs and the choral dancing were particularly remarkable. First came *Oklahoma* with dances arranged by the imaginative Agnes de Mille. Then followed *Annie get your Gun* and many others. You would probably recognize the songs from most of them. 'Oh, what a beautiful morning' and 'Doin' what comes naturally' are two of them. Could you add more to a list of these musicals and song titles?

A shot from the film
West Side Story.

The most revolutionary of them all from a dancing point of view
was *West Side Story* (1957) with choreography by Jerome
Robbins. Each member of the chorus was a dancer in his or her
own right, with a zing and energy that were electrifying, and the

Another scene from
West Side Story.

dancing had become more realistic and connected to life as it is lived. Practically all these musicals started in the theatre and were then made into films that are revived from time to time. Try to see them if possible, paying particular attention to the dancing. Quite often a local film society will consider suggestions for films to be shown in the following season, especially if the requests are signed by several people.

Today

There are fewer musicals today and they are seldom on such a large scale. One reason is that a great spectacular musical is a very costly affair. If it is not a big success, enormous sums of money are lost.

It has become more practical to produce dancing on television. Owing to this a whole new technique has evolved. The 'takes' are not cut, repeated and rearranged as in a cinema film. Instead of performing to a single mass of spectators, as in a theatre, the dancers are moving in front of about five differently placed moveable cameras and have to take that fact into consideration. Next time you watch a dance programme *especially designed for television* notice where the various view points have been used to advantage and where they may have presented difficulties.

Among the special television 'jazz' dance companies that have arisen are Pan's People (recently retired), The Young Generation and New Edition.

7 Classical ballet

Is ballet different?

Glamour and hard slog

What has to be learnt and where to learn it

We come now to the queen of dancing, classical ballet. Pictures of ballet abound. Illustrations of new ballets appear in the press, local ballet schools display photographs of their star pupils, and it is a favourite subject for artists. A French painter, Edgar Degas (1834–1917) is the most famous. He was connected with the painters known as the Impressionists and his lovely but realistic studies of dancers on stage or in class are often reproduced in books or on postcards. The latter could form an interesting collection.

Some of the originals can be seen at London's Tate Gallery and the Art Gallery and museum at Kelvingrove in Glasgow. Pictures of dancers by other famous painters such as Breughel and Watteau could be added.

Classical and romantic
Classical is one of those words we use without really thinking about them — and it *is* rather difficult to pin down, because its meaning varies. It usually describes a kind of art based on outside rules that have proved their worth over many years, or else a work that is still appreciated and valued after a long time. We apply it, too, to ancient Greece and Rome to indicate that we are not referring to those places in later periods.

Sometimes the term 'romantic' is used as its opposite, to describe a work of art that follows its creator's inner feelings rather than general rules of excellence.

The difference

What, then, distinguishes classical ballet from other dancing? One might say it was a sort of stage dancing founded on certain rules first laid down over three hundred years ago. The most basic of these rules is that the legs must be turned out from the hips, which means that knees and feet also turn outwards. Notice this point next time you see ballet, or pictures of it.

The existence of this rule has been explained in a number of ways. It is merely an exaggeration of the style used in seventeenth-century social dancing, some say, which was made necessary by the wide-topped boots worn by the men. Whether that is true or not, there is no doubt that the position gives better balance and control as well as a more airborne grace. At first the feet were only turned out at an angle of 45° but by 1830 that had become 90°. There are five foot positions as illustrated. Try standing in them yourself, with legs turned out as described.

The 'turnout' and the five foot positions.

Finding out about ballet

As with all the arts, and sport as well, the more you know about ballet, the more you enjoy watching it. A ballet is not only dancing. It is a unity made up of three elements: dance, music and décor — that is to say set and costumes.

Professional companies tour the country much more than they used to, but there are considerable difficulties: expense, a suitable theatre, questions of audience. Think out what the expenses would be and what problems might exist in regard to the last two.

If live ballet cannot visit your neighbourhood, you may be able to see it in the cinema or, more often, on television. You may get a chance to watch a ballet class or an end-of-year display by a ballet school.

Should you have been lucky enough to see a live performance by one of the great ballet companies, you will not have forgotten the final ceremony. The spectacle is over, the huge curtains swing together, a spotlight falls on where they meet. Suddenly the glorious ballerina is there with the chief male dancer beside her. She makes a deep curtsey, he bows. Bouquets of flowers are brought to her and, holding them in her arms she curtseys again. The audience applauds wildly, on and on. The glory and glamour overwhelm us. Oh, to be a ballet dancer!

Behind the scenes

Before we tear off to the nearest ballet school, however, we should reflect that no one becomes expert at anything, be it music, diving or football, without hours and years of patient drudgery — and that is truer of ballet dancing than of almost anything else. A ballet dancer has to lead a dedicated life. So, unless you are prepared for that, it will be better to enjoy it as a knowledgeable spectator and, perhaps, make a project out of it. There are enthusiasts who go to as many ballets as possible and can tell you everything about them. They don't mind how often they see the same ballet, because they can compare the performances or different dancers in the same parts. People like that are called 'balletomanes'.

Ballet clubs

In nearly every large town there is a ballet club that puts on monthly programmes connected with dancing. The small fee charged is very good value. In one season there might be a demonstration by a small section of the Royal Ballet, a display by the top class of a ballet school or an evening of Indian or Spanish dancing, for instance. Many of these clubs also run classes for beginners and more advanced pupils. Although you may never mean to become a professional, a few lessons will enable you to become a much more understanding audience.

The ballet school

Let us look at a school for would-be professional ballet dancers. It must be a good one, for bad teaching can spoil a dancer for ever. Girls should begin serious training at eleven, boys a year or two later. Pupils are carefully selected, and many turned away. Apart from keenness, musicality and talent, they must have the right looks and build, a strong foot and supple back being specially important. Long hands and feet are a sign that a girl may grow taller than the 5 feet 6 inches, considered the limit for female dancers. But there are exceptions to every rule. Some have started training later, several ballerinas are over 5 feet 6 inches, and the famous dancer, Alicia Markova, first took dancing lessons to cure her weak feet.

The practice room is large and bare with bars about 3 feet in height all along the walls. One or two mirrors are there to show the dancers if they are holding themselves properly. The students wear a simple top above footless woollen tights and socks, for cold leg muscles can cause injury. On their feet are ballet shoes which must be of exactly the right kind.

Practice

First the students practise holding on to the 'barre'. All leg movements, whether bending, circling or kicking, must be done with the legs turned out. After this they do exercises in the centre of the room, including jumps and sequences of steps. Legs and feet are not everything. Trunk, head, arms, hands and expression must all be right. The whole body must be in harmony. Even a prima ballerina practises for some three hours a day and may go to a class as well.

Steps and their names

There are a great many steps, all of which can be done in a number of ways, e.g. along the ground or in the air. And all, for reasons that will be explained later, have French names which dancers have to learn. For instance, a *pirouette* is a spin round, an *entrechat* is a spring during which the heels are crossed once or more in the air; an *arabesque* is a graceful attitude in which the body leans forward with one arm outstretched and the opposing leg held out behind. Do you know or can you guess what is meant by *pas-de-deux*, *elevation* and *rond de jambe en l'air*?

The art of mime – that is, words expressed by gesture – is a part of ballet, but much less used to-day. A hundred years ago there was a regular language of mime, e.g. placing the hand on the heart meant 'love'. Could you convey the sentence 'I will pay you to go there' purely in mime?

Technique and art

Although ballet students must do physical exercises every day, they are not allowed to neglect their ordinary lessons. A good dancer needs to know about other things as well as dancing. Technique, that is to say practical skill, is not everything. Dancing becomes great art only when it can convey any shade of meaning or emotion demanded of it, with a technique so perfected that it is never obvious.

Men and boys

In Britain and America there is still a lingering feeling that the profession of ballet dancing is not very masculine, which is ridiculous when one remembers that most of the older dances were for men, and that ballet requires at least as much strength and energy as any sport. Ballet exercise is often used for training footballers nowadays, and a still photograph frequently catches them in wonderfully balletic poses.

The idea works as a vicious circle. Boys do not go in for ballet for fear of being thought unmanly. Consequently there are not enough manly boys in British and American Ballet. In Russia and Denmark people think otherwise, and therefore Russian and

Danish companies are famed for their fine male dancers. What do you feel about this situation?

The male dancer usually starts his career as a member of the corps-de-ballet (meaning the main body of the ballet and pronounced 'core de ballay'), what might be called the chorus if it were a musical comedy. Later he may take 'character' parts or become a principal dancer. Part of the latter's task is to support the ballerina in the most helpful and graceful way possible, but sooner or later he will get his turn and give a dazzling display of leaps and turns.

The ballerina
A girl also begins in the corps-de-ballet and may well remain there all her dancing life, a skilled and important part of the whole. She may possibly rise to be a soloist and finally a ballerina. Prima ballerina is an Italian term meaning first female dancer.

A ballet company
Dancers alone do not make a ballet company. A ballet master (*maître de ballet*) or mistress must oversee and train them. Musicians are needed to compose or arrange the music and there is usually an orchestra to play it. Set, costumes and lighting have to be designed by an artist and carried out by painters, scenebuilders, dressmakers and technicians. A host of people are helping behind the scenes.

Perhaps the most important person of all is the choreographer, who plans and directs a ballet, inventing all the steps and grouping, and knowing something about all aspects of a production. Good choreographers are very rare and we need more of them. It is difficult for promising young choreographers to get an opportunity to try out their skill. What special gifts, qualities and sorts of knowledge are needed to make a good choreographer, do you think?

Notation
The way a famous ballet is danced is knowledge passed on from one generation of dancers to the next. But directors have always

wanted to find a surer way and many methods of 'notation' have been invented. It is a complicated business to write down a whole series of changing positions of all the moving parts of a single dancer, let alone a constantly shifting company. Filmed ballet can be useful, though not quite enough in itself.

Idea for a project
If you are clever with your needle you could make a tutu — that is the name of a modern ballerina's frilly little skirt — either for yourself or doll-size. See the illustration.

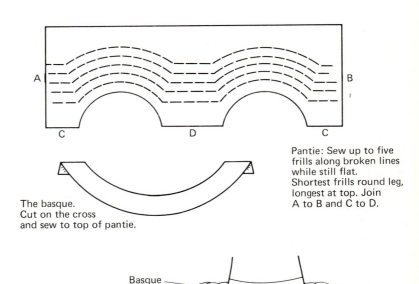

Pantie: Sew up to five frills along broken lines while still flat. Shortest frills round leg, longest at top. Join A to B and C to D.

The basque. Cut on the cross and sew to top of pantie.

Basque

Tutu made of tarlatan, organdie or stiffened net. Wear bodice over basque.

How to make a tutu.

The development of ballet

8

Ballet at the Sun King's court

White tarlatan and moonlight

The Russian Ballet

Before ballet
Dancing to an audience did not begin with pure ballet, of course. Many a grand ball, feast or wedding party was enlivened with a magnificent entertainment partly or wholly made up of dancing. Sixteenth-century Italy was especially fond of these displays, and an Italian princess, Catherine de' Medici, brought the fashion to France when she became queen of that country.

At that date England was famed for her masques, court entertainments that were a mixture of music, singing, dancing and spectacle. A masque might represent, for example, the seasons of the year arriving with their followers to greet an important visitor from abroad. Can you think of a good subject for a masque and how you could bring dancing into it?

Ballet is born
True classical ballet first appeared at the court of the French King Louis XIV, already mentioned in Chapter 4. In 1661 he founded the National Academy of Dance which laid down rules and standards of good dancing. That is why so many ballet terms are in French. They remain so to this day because, with so international an art, it is convenient to use directions that dancers of all nationalities can understand. What helps ballet to be so international in its appeal? What arts, would you say, are less easy to export to foreign lands?

Huge amounts of money were spent on the royal ballets. The best composers wrote the music; scenery and costumes were splendid.

47

The Sun King.
Louis XIV
in a ballet.

Perhaps the weakest department was the dancing itself. At first it
was mainly done by the courtiers. The king himself took part when
young, only playing very grand and dignified roles, of course. Men

took the female parts and the steps were those danced at court balls. So cumbersome were the clothes and headdresses that it was difficult to spring about or turn the head quickly.

Soon, however, professional and female dancers were introduced. Amateurs were out and dancing began to develop.

One famous woman dancer called Camargo shocked and delighted the audience in around 1720 by appearing in a skirt several inches shorter than the usual sweeping court dresses to

Mademoiselle Camargo dancing, *painted by Lancret in the eighteenth century.*

show her pretty ankles and enable her to spring in the air and perform an entrechat.

Jean-Georges Noverre, a Swiss-born dancer and ballet master, wanted to reform ballet in many ways and in 1760 published a book called *Letters on Dancing* which is still considered apt and important to this day. Garrick, the famous English actor, called him the Shakespeare of the Dance.

The era of romance
The 'romantic movement' was fashionable in all the arts during the

early nineteenth century. Moonlit groves, Gothic ruins, desolate crags, hopeless love, enchanters and spirits were all the rage. Ballet was no exception.

Can you find any works of art of that date and in your district that show this 'romantic' taste — pictures, poems, above all architecture?

One of the earliest romantic ballets was *La Sylphide* (not to be confused with the later *Les Sylphides*). It was about a fairy-like spirit who fell in love with a Scottish nobleman just before his wedding day. The sylph, danced by the adored Marie Taglioni, wore a tight-waisted, full-skirted white dress reaching a few inches below her knee. Though it was, in fact, just a shortened version of an 1830–40 ball gown, it has since become the typical ballet dress.

The position of prima ballerinas in those days was comparable to that of pop stars today. Students would unhitch the horses from Taglioni's carriage and draw it home from the theatre themselves.

Taglioni would make a good subject for a biographical sketch. She was trained by her father, who made her practice relentlessly until she was nearly exhausted — only to appear that evening, a miracle of seemingly effortless airborne grace.

Giselle (1841), still danced today, is another ballet of the romantic period. It was during this time that dancing on the 'points' began, and that feet were turned out at an angle of 90°.

A model stage
An interesting addition to a ballet project, if you are good with your hands and artistic, would be a model theatre. It could be a team effort. Get the stage proportions right. It need only be a simple framework to support scenery and figures that you have painted and cut out. Interesting lighting effects could be obtained with electric torches and coloured cellophane.

A less ambitious effort would be to dress a small figure or doll in the typical ballet dress described above. What sort of hair-do goes with it?

Top nations
It is interesting to see how supremacy in ballet passes from one country to another. The leading nation sends its experts to teach abroad and only slowly is it realized that its own ballet, by clinging too long to the very rules that brought success, has grown stale and set in its ways. Then, perhaps, in one of the countries that nation helped to teach, ballet rises up again vital and vivid, reigns supreme for a while and finally degenerates in its turn. Can you think of other spheres — of art, science or sport — where the same thing happens?

Thus France sent dancing teachers to Italy and Denmark, and later on ballet masters from the flourishing ballet companies in each of these countries were invited to visit Russia.

Russia
They were sent for because the emperors, or czars, of Russia during the seventeenth and eighteenth centuries wanted to westernize their vast country. Among other measures they imported ballet. The Russians took to it like ducks to water. Before many years had passed there was a flourishing school of dance attached to the grand Imperial Ballet at the Maryinsky theatre in St Petersburg, then Russia's capital. After the Revolution the city's name was changed. Do you know what it is called today? Another great ballet company was founded in Moscow.

The Maryinsky days
The St Petersburg ballet was supported by the czar, so could afford to put on magnificent productions. To our modern eyes some of the scenery and costumes of the late nineteenth century look too fussy. Many of the ballets were mere fairy stories accompanied by trivial music and intended only to show off the ballerinas. But the dancing was superb, due partly to the great Italian teacher of dance, Cecchetti, and the choreography of the famous *maître de ballet* Marius Petipa — and we must not forget that celebrated composers such as Tchaikowsky and Glazounov were sometimes commissioned to write music for the ballet.

The former composed the music of three of the most famous 'classical' ballets. They are so described because they kept to traditional values and have survived on account of their excel-

Petrouchka, a Diaghilev ballet. Choreography by Fokine, music by Stravinsky, designed by Benois. Margot Fonteyn is dancing the doll puppet.

lence. But their subject matter could hardly be more romantic! Perhaps Tchaikowsky's masterpiece was *Swan Lake*, first performed in 1877. It was not a success when first produced and the composer died in 1893 still under the impression that it was a failure.

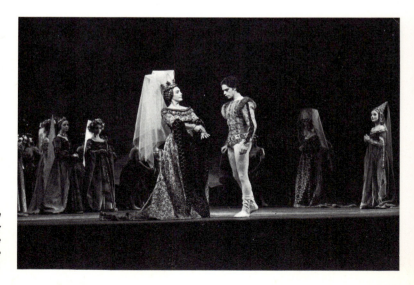

A mime scene from Swan Lake *danced by the Royal Ballet. The Queen tells the Prince he must marry.*

Do you know the names of his other two ballets? If you play the records of their music you are sure to recognize some of it.

The stalls at the Maryinsky Theatre glittered with diamonds, and the czar himself with his relations, the grand dukes, were often there to watch their favourite ballerinas. They might, indeed, have been called the Stage Door Johnnies of the Imperial Ballet.

Diaghilev
The Russian Serge Diaghilev was possibly the greatest impresario that ever lived. An impresario is a person who knows about an art but does not practise it himself. Instead he organizes and displays artists and their work. Can you think of similar positions today?

Diaghilev was at first more interested in music and painting. When his interest turned to dancing there were already a number of people who felt that ballet needed reform. Under his leadership they broke away from the Imperial Company and in 1909/10 toured western Europe with Russian opera and ballet.

The genius of Diaghilev lay in recognizing and drawing out the genius of others. What names were listed in his company! Stravinsky composed for him; Bakst, Benois and later Picasso designed sets and costumes. Among his dancers were Massine,

HINTS TO CLIMBERS: HOW TO ATTRACT NOTICE.
I. WEAR COSTUMES DESIGNED BY M. LÉON BAKST, WHO, WE HEAR, IS ADDING TO HIS TRIUMPHS IN THE FIELD OF RUSSIAN BALLET BY CREATING MODELS FOR A PARISIAN MODISTE.

Making fun of fashions inspired by the Diaghilev Ballet.

Pavlova and Nijinsky of the great leaps, who tragically went insane and never danced again, as well as the beautiful Karsavina who, as I write, still lives, a charming aged lady, in Hampstead.

Pavlova
Anna Pavlova did not stay long in the group. She formed her own company and toured the world many times before her death in 1931. Although the music, décor and main company were considered inferior to those of the Diaghilev Ballet, she herself was unequalled. Her solo dance *The Dying Swan* inspired a whole generation of young dancers and, in a way, her influence on ballet has been as great as that of the famous impresario.

Fokine
Perhaps the most important member of Diaghilev's company was Michel Fokine, dancer and choreographer. He felt that a ballet should be an equal partnership of subject, music, design and dancing, a unity created together, whereas in the Imperial ballet these aspects were often carried out independently and unrelated to one another. In such ideas he went back to Noverre.

Do you consider that these four elements are equally important in a ballet, or that only the dancing really matters? It is a very old argument.

Success
Ballet in the rest of Europe was in decline, seen only as a part of opera, or a pretty-pretty entertainment in which the men's parts were danced by women.

In any case, the new ballets were immensely exciting. All the intellectuals and artists of Europe were talking about the barbaric splendour of Bakst's colours, the strangeness of Stravinsky's music, the fire and perfection of the dancing. The designs influenced not only the theatre but also fashions in clothes and interior decoration.

Among their ballets still sometimes danced today are *Les Sylphides*, *Petrouchka* and *Firebird*. The company also performed the classical ballets from the Imperial era. When you make a list of ballets you should always mention the choreographer, composer, designer, date of first production and, if possible, the subject.

A riot

The success story was not uninterrupted, however. Diaghilev had enemies and in 1913, when he produced *Rite of Spring*, they thought it was too revolutionary. Nijinsky, who had done the choreography, made the dancers turn their feet in instead of out, and many critics considered Stravinsky's music hideously modern. In Paris, at the first performance, there was a riot. The part of the audience who were against the ballet shouted and threw things. You can at least judge the music for yourselves, for since then it has been used in part of Disney's film *Fantasia*. The original plot was a spring ritual in ancient, pagan Russia, including the sacrifice of a maiden. After seeing the film we are more likely to be reminded of spinning planets, exploding volcanoes and dinosaurs dying in the wilderness.

Take one ballet

An interesting exercise would be a study of one famous ballet: story or subject, choreography, music, decor, its first performance and subsequent history, the dancers who starred in it, and so on. Suitable works would be *Giselle* (1841), *Coppelia* (1870), *Petrouchka* (1911). It would be best to choose a ballet you have a chance of seeing.

Or could you think of a ballet theme, choose music for it and work out at least a vague idea of how it should look?

An end and a beginning

In 1929 Diaghilev suddenly died. His wonderful company broke up and formed splinter groups in various parts of the world. Most of them were unsuccessful but enriched the soil for future ballet.

9

Ballet today

Upheavals in Russia

England's turn

Ballet spreads far and wide

And develops

Nineteen-seventeen was the year of the Russian Revolution. The czar was deposed and killed with all his family, but the Imperial ballets survived, now supported by the state. The Maryinsky Theatre changed its name to the Kirov, while the Moscow company continued to dance at the enormous Bolshoi Theatre (*bolshoi* is Russian for great). The standard of dancing remains as high as ever — possibly the highest in the world — although in some other respects they have been surpassed by the western ballet companies. These two great Russian groups very occasionally tour in Europe and America, always acting as a tonic to the dancers there.

A beautiful arabesque by Antoinette Sibley with Anthony Dowell. The Royal Ballet's Swan Lake.

Diaghilev's legacy

After Diaghilev's death remnants of his troupe with some fresh additions remained at Monte Carlo, which had long been his headquarters. They formed a series of ballet companies which, under various names and directors, carried on for many years.

Some of Diaghilev's dancers were English, although at that time they had to use Russian names. Among them were Sokolova, Anton Dolin and Alicia Markova. Can you find out their real names? Anglo-Irish Ninette de Valois belongs to the same group, except that her adopted name is French. These four, together with Marie Rambert, a Polish dancer married to an Englishman, returned to England, where ballet was in a very poor state. Between them they revived the dying flame. The story of how this country was restored to her former dancing eminence is quite a cliff-hanger.

Early struggles

There was very little money to spend, not much organizing experience, and an uncaring public to be won over. Both Marie Rambert and Ninette de Valois had opened ballet schools. Devotees of ballet organized a few dance recitals. In 1930 the Rambert school took over the tiny Mercury Theatre in London and produced interesting ballets on a small scale, such as *Façade* choreographed by a young dancer called Frederick Ashton. De Valois pupils sometimes put on ballets at a shabby theatre called the Old Vic, which later became . . . do you know what?

In 1931 Ninette was asked to transfer her school to Sadler's Wells Theatre, a beautiful little place, just re-opened after many years, and to produce ballets there about once a fortnight. Soon they became much more frequent.

So British ballet put down roots. At first its life was often in danger through lack of money.

Dolin and Markova danced at Sadler's Wells from 1932 to 1935 when they founded their own company. Some delightful ballets were created by de Valois, e.g. *The Rake's Progress* which followed the story of Hogarth's series of paintings so named, which can be seen at the Soane Museum in London. Later

Frederick Ashton, now considered one of the world's greatest choreographers, joined the company. Youthful but gifted dancers began to emerge, Margot Fonteyn and Robert Helpmann among them.

It was an amazing success story. The audience grew in numbers and brilliance and the atmosphere tingled with excitement. One never knew what fascinating ballet or promising dancer would next appear.

Lesley Collier of the Royal Ballet does a pigeon step in Les Deux Pigeons.

Success

After the war in 1946, Sadler's Wells Ballet moved to the splendid Covent Garden Opera House, which it still shares with the Royal

Opera Company. Three years later its name was changed to the Royal Ballet. By now it was a much larger and richer company and tended to produce more of the full-length classical ballets, though new and shorter pieces are not excluded. A small company in a modest theatre can risk experiment with more safety. Can you see why this is?

Belonging to the Royal Ballet are various daughter groups: the smaller company with headquarters at Sadler's Wells; Ballet for All, a small group that tours the country and gives demonstrations; and the new experimental division. Even the big company tours every year.

Other British ballets

It is far from being the only ballet company in the British Isles, however. There are also the Festival, Scottish, New London, and Irish ballets. The last three are fairly new enterprises.

A good subject for a study would be the history of one of the older companies such as the Sadler's Wells or Ballet Rambert. One would have to find out their stories, names of production (with dates), choreographers, ballerinas, etc., and read reviews and accounts of their ballets, find music, programmes, photographs and so on.

One of our most distinguished choreographers is Kenneth MacMillan. Listen to the forceful yet haunting theme that opens Prokoviev's music for his ballet of *Romeo and Juliet*. Until recently MacMillan was also director of the Royal Ballet. He found the immense work of administration left him no time for his artistic career. Now he has retired to devote himself to choreography. His successor is Norman Morrice, formerly director of Ballet Rambert.

Among our best dancers are Antoinette Sibley, Lynn Seymour and David Wall, but there are many others. It would be fine if you could spot the rising stars yourself.

Do you know the name of the splendid young dancer who left the Kirov Ballet in 1961 and starred for some time at Covent Garden Opera House? People would wait in queues all night to see him and Margot Fonteyn as partners there, and he still dances in England from time to time.

Nureyev leaping.

Ballet abroad

I have dwelt mainly on British ballet because it is a very much easier subject for *local search*. Of course there are splendid companies and dancers abroad too. One of the world's greatest choreographers is George Balanchine, who was once in Diaghilev's Company and now directs the New York City Ballet. Other important choreographers are the American Jerome Robbins and Hans Van Mahen of the Netherlands.

Cinema and TV

When a film is made out of a stage ballet such as *Romeo and Juliet* the director has several problems to face. Should he shoot the whole performance as if seen from a seat in the theatre? Should he take close-ups of the principal dancers, thus missing the rest of the company? He can at least photograph the same scene from different angles. Moreover, a film is a record of dance and dancer impossible to earlier centuries.

It is easier to film a ballet designed for the cinema from the start, as were *The Red Shoes* and *Tales of Beatrix Potter*. *I am a Dancer*, the

Nureyev film, is one you should see. It illustrates so many points touched on in this book. Television ballet gives rise to even greater problems because of the tiny screen. However, Robert Cohan of the London Contemporary Dance Theatre composed a magically beautiful ballet called *Men Seen Afar* especially for television. It could not be danced in a theatre.

Schools and subsidies

There are numerous ballet schools in this country, some better than others, the Royal Ballet School being the most renowned. You can find out about many of them from the fascinating advertisements in the *Dancing Times* and similar magazines.

Today's high prices and wages make it very expensive to stage a play. How much more so to run a ballet company, which has to have a whole repertory of different ballets, a great number of dancers and staff, costly sets and costumes and an orchestra! No ballet company of any size can hope to make a continuous profit.

In the old days ballet and opera were either financed by monarchs and rich patrons or they went bankrupt. Now it is the state that helps with subsidies, money that comes from the taxpayer. I wonder if you know the name of the organisation responsible for arranging these subsidies? Some people grumble, saying that ballet should pay its way or close. On the other hand, it attracts many tourists, bringing money into the country. Moreover, it is a source of pride to the nation, which might well be ashamed to let a great art die for lack of a few pence a year per inhabitant. What are your views on that question? .

Experiment

There are other reasons besides cost, however, why abstract ballets are so popular. Is a story more essential to ballet than to music? An abstract ballet has no plot or definite location. It may express a mood, an idea, or simply be a composition of moving figures.

Experiment in art is healthy. But where one artist creates something truly original because he feels that is the way it has to be, others will jump on the bandwagon and produce shallow novelty for fashion's sake. There is a continual tug-of-war between tradition and experiment.

If every change were a vast improvement on what went before, as we sometimes tend to feel at the time, our art today would be enormously better than the best of past centuries. Is it? And if things were never as good as they used to be, the present time would be vastly inferior to the Stone Age.

Modern dance

10

Reaction against ballet

Natural movement

Great personalities

Extremes begin to meet

It is not always possible to be sure where a new invention or movement really starts. There is 'something in the air' that makes the same idea occur to more than one person at the same time.

In this way, around 1900, a reaction against classical ballet set in, giving rise to theories of natural dance movement in both America and Central Europe. Today these ideas have been put into action and merged to form what we now call Modern or Contemporary Dance.

Isadora
The American pioneer was Isadora Duncan (1878–1927). You may have seen the film of her dramatic life. She was strongly against classical ballet with its turnout, point work and fixed steps. Ancient Greek dancing was the model for her own system of movements to express emotion and interpret music. She danced in bare feet and soft draperies. Although she appeared to move on the inspiration of the moment, she did in fact practise and rehearse a great deal.

Unappreciated in her own country, she came to Europe, where her genius was received with open arms. She gave performances and also ran a school to teach her methods and spread her ideas.

Central Europe
Meanwhile Rudolf Laban, a Hungarian, was working out a new

theory of dancing and of notation to record its movements. He, too, founded a school, the influence of which is still powerful today. He finally settled in England.

One of his pupils was Kurt Jooss, a fine dancer himself, who created some very interesting modern ballets. Best known was *The Green Table*, a satire on war and its aftermath. You may be able to find a photograph of its strange, masked dancers. Jooss left Germany because he disagreed with Hitler's policies and taught in England during the war.

Martha Graham
Another American woman of genius has perhaps had the greatest influence of all on Modern Dance. She is Martha Graham, who ran a dance company and school in New York for many years. They still thrive. It has been said that her dancers are 'thought and emotion in action' and 'alive in every limb'. Among her greatest ballets are *Clytemnestra* and *Deaths and Entrances*. Can you find out any more about her?

As it is now
All these pioneers have contributed to dancing as it is today. There are companies and schools of Modern Dance all over the world, especially in the USA. The best known in Britain is the London Contemporary Dance Theatre. Rambert Ballet now specializes in Modern Dance. The newest venture, as I write, is the Welsh Dance Theatre in Cardiff.

In this type of dancing the legs are not always turned out and there is no point work. Movement must spread from the centre of the body outwards, and its relation to the ground is as important as its position in the air. You will notice that in Modern Dance a great deal of the action takes place lying or half-lying on the floor. 'We make use of gravity ... the spine should be like a snake', says Robert Cohan, director of the London Contemporary Dance Theatre. Where do you see differences between these principles and those of classical ballet?

The setting of a modern ballet is often very spare or absent, leaving a bare, black stage illuminated by moving shafts of light. The

Ballet Rambert: Echoes of a Night Sky.

lighting effects can be very beautiful. To show movements more clearly the costume usually consists of plain body-fitting leotards. Sometimes conventional music is used. Quite as often the dancing is accompanied by drum beats, speech or even silence. Subject matter is frequently rather gloomy.

The aim may be pure dance, a moving pattern of human bodies with no distractions. This is a long way from Fokine's idea of ballet as an equal union of the arts.

It is the present fashion, but some people think it has become too 'puritanical'. Are we missing something valuable when ballet has no splendour of sound or scene, no curtain to reveal a surprise? What is your opinion?

Exercises

If you are interested in the feeling of Modern Dance, try this exercise for two or more people. To the accompaniment of suitable music or rhythmic sounds two dancers stand erect. Then dancer A slowly 'expands'; spine stretching upwards, arms outwards, face looking up. At the same time dancer B gradually 'shrinks' until curled up in a compressed shape on the floor. After a certain number of bars they change roles, B gradually stretching outwards as A curls up.

See if you can express some everyday activity such as cleaning a
room or playing cricket in terms of Modern Dance.

Learning from each other

When the first rebels turned against classical ballet the two types
of dancer were mortal enemies. The enthusiasts for change called
the classical style rigid and artificial. The ballet dancers despised
the other side as under-trained amateurs who made themselves
look ridiculous through lack of proper training.

Now the situation is rather different. Each side has realized it has
something to learn from the other. Dancers of the modern school
now all do classical ballet training as well as their own because it
provides the best basis for dance movement, and they sometimes
use classical techniques in their ballets. Certain of the ballets now
danced by the classical companies are almost indistinguishable
from Contemporary Dance. Although the two types still hold
themselves very separate, they are growing nearer and each has
enriched the other.

Further reading and useful addresses

General
Encyclopaedia Britannica: see Micropedia under 'Dance'.
Raffé, W. G., *Dictionary of the Dance*, Yoseloff, 1964.
Scholes, P. A., ed., *The Oxford Companion to Music*, Oxford University Press, 10th edition, 1970 (also describes dances).
Sharp, Cecil, and Oppé, A. P., *The Dance*, E.P. Publishing, 1972.

Folk and national
Alford, Violet, ed., *Handbooks of European National Dances*, Max Parrish, 1948.
Anderton, A., *A Complete Guide to Scottish Dancing*, Collins, 1972.
Blake, Lois, *The Welsh Folk Dance*, Gwynne, Llangollen.
Blake, Lois, *Welsh Folk Dancing and Costume*, Gwynne, Llangollen.
Duggan, A., *Folk Dances of the British Isles*, Barnes, New York, 1948.
Kennedy, Douglas, *English Folk Dancing of Today and Yesterday*, Bell, 1949.
Lawler, L. B., *The Dance in Ancient Greece*, A. & C. Black, 1964.
Lawson, Joan, *European Folk Dance*, Pitman, 1970.
Sharp, Cecil, and Milligan, J. C., *The Sword Dances of Northern England*, E.P. Publishing, 1977.
Sharp, Cecil, and Butterworth, George, *The Country Dance Book* (4 parts), E.P. Publishing, 1975.
Sharp, Cecil, and McIluraine, A., *The Morris Book*, E.P. Publishing, 1977.

Social and historical
Franks, A. H., *Social Dance*, Routledge & Kegan Paul, 1963.
Guthrie, J., *Historical Dances for the Theatre*, Aldridge, 1950.
Wood, Melusine, *Historical Dances from the 12th to the 19th Centuries*, Imperial Society of Dancing Teachers, 1964.

Ballroom and stage

Borrows, F., *Latin American Dance Book*, Muller, 1964.

Engel, L. K., *The Fred Astaire Dance Book*, Souvenir Press, 1962.

Fairley, R., *Come Dancing, Miss World*, Newman Neame, 1966.

McNair, R. J., *Square Dance*, W. H. Allen, 1952.

Silvester, Victor, *Modern Ballroom Dancing*, Barrie & Jenkins, 1964.

Silvester, Victor and Whitman, Walter, *The Complete Old Time Dancer*, Herbert Jenkins, 1967.

Ballet and modern dance

Ambrose, Kay, *Beginners Please*, A. & C. Black, 1972.

Brinson, Peter and Crisp, Clement, *Ballet for All*, David & Charles, 1970.

Davidson, Gladys, *Stories of the Ballet*, Werner Laurie, 1958.

Guest, Ivor, *The Romantic Ballet in England*, Pitman, 1972.

Guest, Ivor, 'The Dancer's Heritage', *Dancing Times*, 1970.

Jenkins, Jean, *Musical Instruments at the Horniman Museum*, Inner London Education Authority, 1970.

Kerensky, Oleg, *Ballet Scene*, Hamish Hamilton, 1970.

Lawson, Joan, *A History of Ballet and its Makers*, Dance Books, 1973.

Moldon, P. L., *Your Book of Ballet*, Faber & Faber, 1974.

Roslavleva, Natalia, *Era of the Russian Ballet*, Gollancz, 1966.

Rowell, Kenneth, *Stage Design*, Studio Vista, 1971.

Searle, Humphrey, *Ballet Music*, Constable, 1958.

Wilson, G. B. L., *A Dictionary of Ballet*, Cassell, 1961.

Magazines and journals

Ballroom Dancing Times (monthly)

Dance and Dancers (ballet, modern, etc., monthly)

Dancing Times (ballet, modern, etc., monthly)

English Dance and Song (folk quarterly)

Useful addresses

The English Folk Dance and Song Society, Cecil Sharp House, 2 Regents Park Road, London NW1.

Mr John Dillworth, General Secretary of the International

Association of Ballet Clubs, The Honorary Secretary, 51 Vartry Road, South Tottenham, London N15.

A catalogue of folk dance music can be obtained from: Novello & Co., 27 Soho Square, London W1.

Records of foreign and other folk dance music can be obtained from: Discurio, 9 Shepherd Street, London W1.

Note: Remember to send a stamped addressed envelope with postal enquiries except to national institutions.

Acknowledgments

The author and publishers would like to thank those listed below for permission to reproduce illustrations on the pages listed: the Trustees of the British Museum, pp. 3 and 6; the Indonesian Embassy, p. 8; the Nigeria High Commission, p. 9; the Irish Tourist Board, p. 13; the *Herts Advertiser*, pp. 16 and 19; Charles Woolfe, p. 17; Lensman Photos Ltd, p. 23; Viscount de L'Isle, VC, KG, p. 25; London Borough of Southwark, p. 27; *Punch*, pp. 28 and 53; Jack Blake, pp. 33 and 34; Metro-Goldwyn-Mayer Films Ltd, p. 37; United Artists Corporation Ltd, p. 38; Harvey James, pp. 41 and 46; the Bibliothèque Nationale, p. 48; the Wallace Collection, p. 49; G. B. L. Wilson, pp. 52, 56, 58 and 60; Anthony Crickmay, pp. ii–iii and 65.

The author gratefully acknowledges the help of Miss Molly DuCane; Mr Lewis Budd; Mrs Marguerita Hoare; Mr Alan Newcombe and Mrs Irene Newcombe; Mr G. B. L. Wilson and Miss Ruth Pearson of 'Pan's People'.

70

The local search series

Editor: Mrs Molly Harrison MBE, FRSA

This book is one of a highly successful series designed to help young people to look inquiringly and critically at particular aspects of the world about them. It encourages them to think for themselves, to seek first-hand information from other people, to make the most of visits to interesting places, and to record their discoveries and their experiences.

Many boys and girls enjoy detective work of this kind and find it fun to look for evidence and to illustrate their findings in ways that appeal to them. Such lively activities are equally rewarding whether carried out individually or in a group.